PIANO | VOCAL | GUITAR

blues&soul
CHRISTMAS

ISBN 978-1-4234-5682-7

CORPORATION
7777 W. BLUEMOUND RD. P.O. BOX 13819 MILWAUKEE, WI 53213

Visit Hal Leonard Online at
www.halleonard.com

ALL ALONE ON CHRISTMAS

from the Twentieth Century Fox Motion Picture HOME ALONE 2

By STEVEN VAN ZANDT

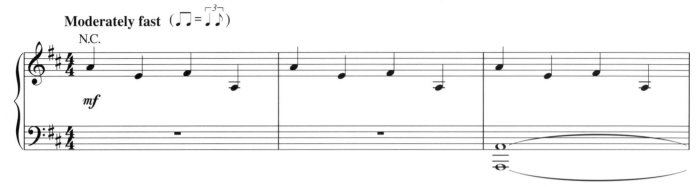

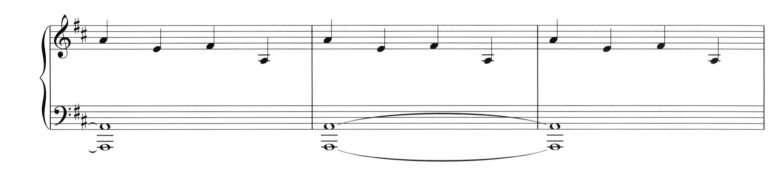

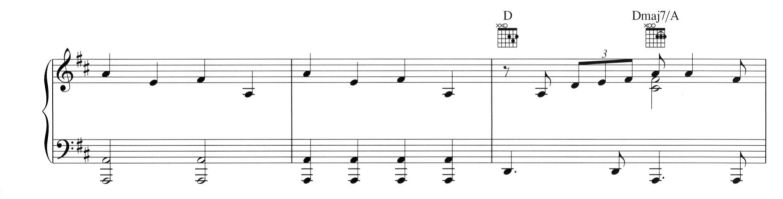

BACK DOOR SANTA

Words and Music by MARCUS LEWIS DANIEL
and CLARENCE GEORGE CARTER

Moderate Funk

They

call me Back _ Door San - ta,
ain't like old _ Saint Nick, _____

I make my runs _ a - bout the break of
he don't come _____ but _ once a

BABY, IT'S COLD OUTSIDE

from the Motion Picture NEPTUNE'S DAUGHTER

By FRANK LOESSER

BLUE CHRISTMAS

Words and Music by BILLY HAYES
and JAY JOHNSON

Moderately

I'll have a blue Christ-mas, with-out you._____ I'll be so

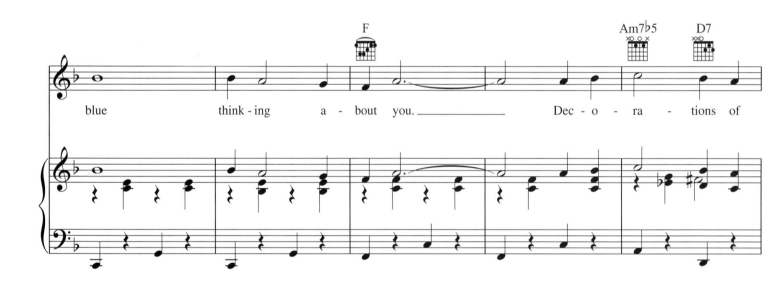

blue think-ing a-bout you._____ Dec-o-ra-tions of

red on a green Christ-mas tree won't mean a thing if

BOOGIE WOOGIE SANTA CLAUS

Words and Music by
LEON RENE

Well, look-ee here, Jack, there's some-thin' down the track, he got rhy-thm in his feet but noth-

To Coda

Mis - ter San - ta. Jump, jump, jump, ___ { Mis - ter San - ta, well, ___
Mis - ter San - ta Claus. ___

Ab7

jump.

F#dim7   Fm7   E9   Fm7   Bb7

Eb

Got no

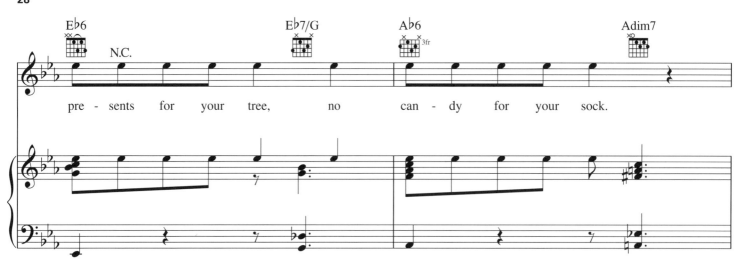

pre - sents for your tree, no can - dy for your sock.

When you start to boog - ie, the whole ____ town rocks.

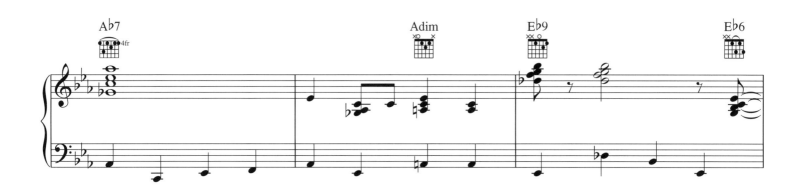

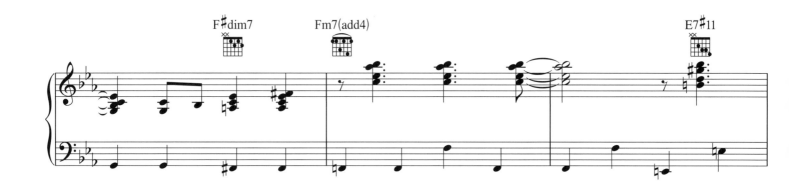

D.S. al Coda

Well, the Boog-ie Woog-ie San-ta will boog-ie all your blues a-way.

CHRISTMAS
(Baby Please Come Home)

Words and Music by PHIL SPECTOR,
ELLIE GREENWICH and JEFF BARRY

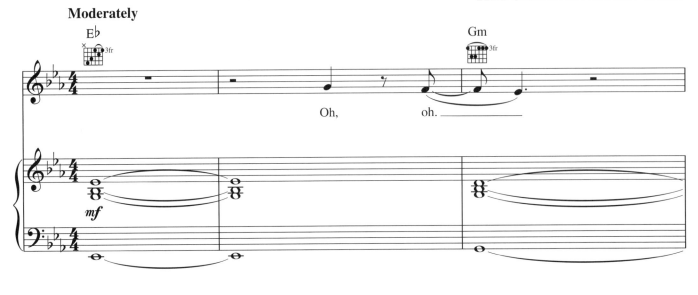

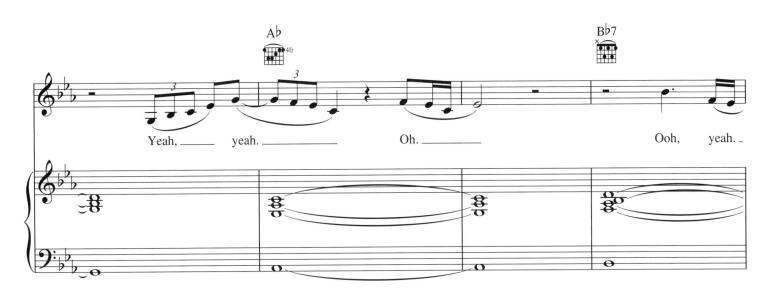

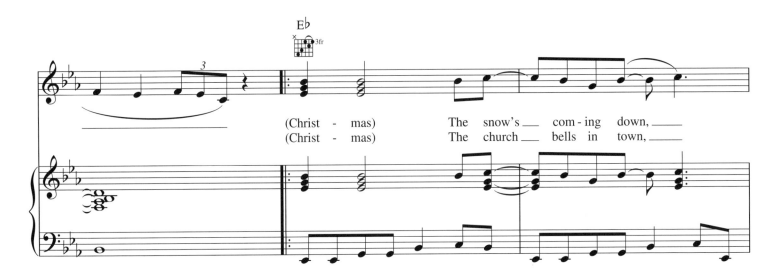

CHRISTMAS BLUES

Words and Music by
D. MOORE

DIG THAT CRAZY SANTA CLAUS

Words and Music by ALBERT JOHNSTON JR.,
LEON RENE and RAFAEL RENE

Medium Bounce tempo, with a beat

Dig that cra-zy San-ta Claus, with his red suit on, dig that walk, that cra-zy talk, man, oh man, he's real-ly gone.

LONESOME CHRISTMAS

Words and Music by
LLOYD GLENN

spend this Christ - mas
2. Jin - gle bells are ring - in',
one seems so hap - py,
go shop - pin', ba - by,

sit - tin' by the
chil - dren play - in'
sea - son's greet - in's
there is one thing

5. *Instrumental solo*

fire with you. ___
out in the snow.
fill the air. ___
I'd like to do.

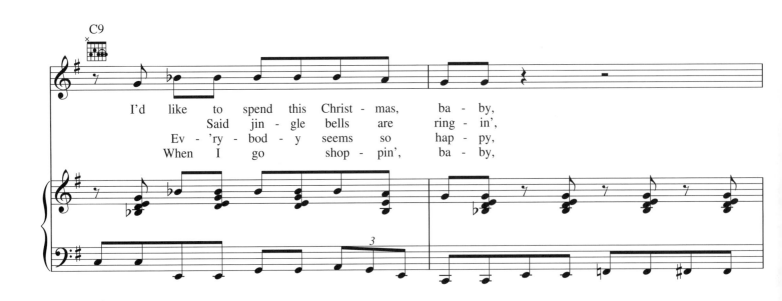

I'd like to spend this Christ - mas, ba - by,
Said jin - gle bells are ring - in',
Ev - 'ry - bod - y seems so hap - py,
When I go shop - pin', ba - by,

GEE WHIZ, IT'S CHRISTMAS

Words and Music by CARLA THOMAS,
STEVE CROPPER and VINCENT TRAUTH

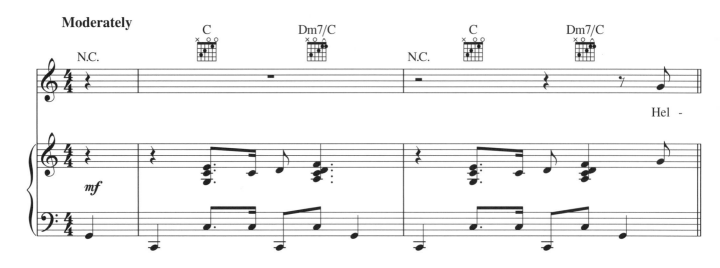

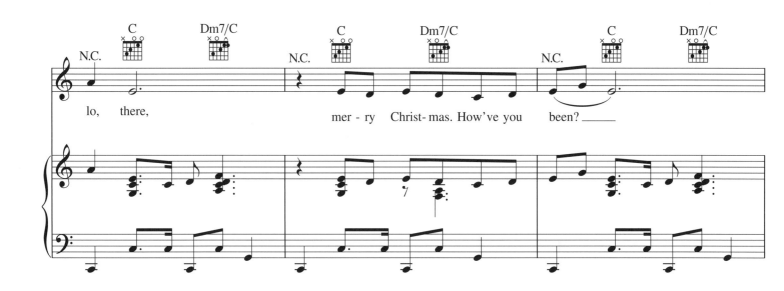

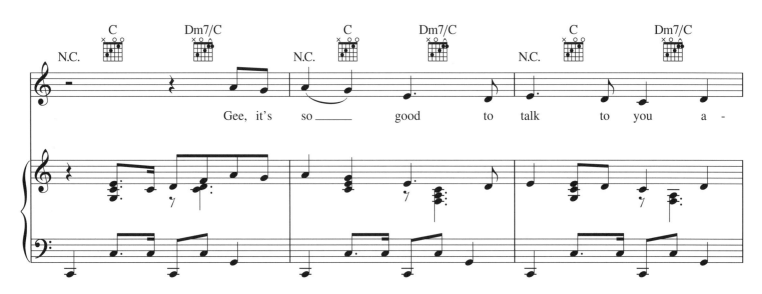

GETTIN' IN THE MOOD
(For Christmas)

Music by JOSEPH GARLAND
Words by BRIAN SETZER
and MICHAEL HIMELSTEIN

I'VE GOT MY LOVE TO KEEP ME WARM

from the 20th Century Fox Motion Picture ON THE AVENUE

Words and Music by
IRVING BERLIN

Bright Jump tempo

JINGLE ALL THE WAY

Words and Music by AL STILLMAN
and RAYMOND ELLIS

Dash-ing through the snow ___ in a one horse o-pen sleigh. ___

___ Laugh-ing as we go, ___

hap-py all the way. 'Round the town we

* Recorded a half step lower.

MERRY CHRISTMAS, BABY

Words and Music by LOU BAXTER
and JOHNNY MOORE

Slow Blues

Instrumental solo ad lib. (2nd time only)

NUTTIN' FOR CHRISTMAS

Words and Music by ROY BENNETT
and SID TEPPER

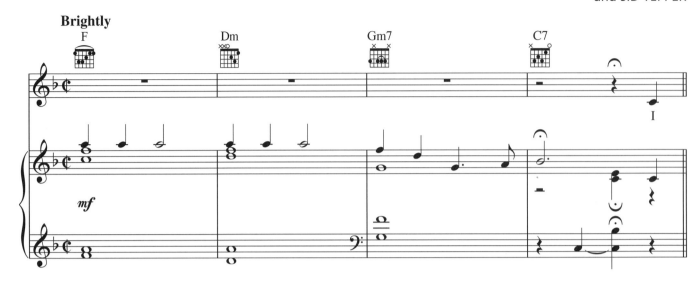

I

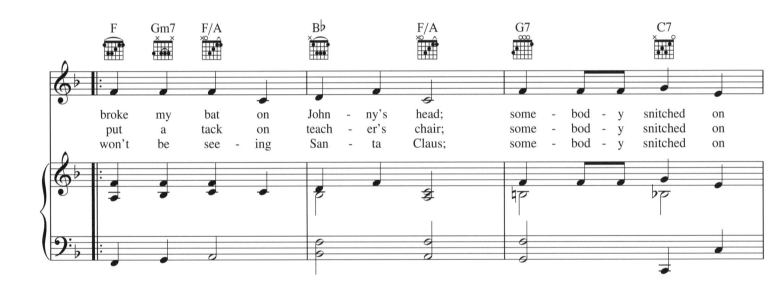

broke my bat on John-ny's head; some-bod-y snitched on
put a tack on teach-er's chair; some-bod-y snitched on
won't be see-ing San-ta Claus; some-bod-y snitched on

me. I hid a frog in sis-ter's bed;
me. I tied a knot in Su-sie's hair;
me. He won't come vis-it me be-cause

PLEASE COME HOME FOR CHRISTMAS

Words and Music by CHARLES BROWN
and GENE REDD

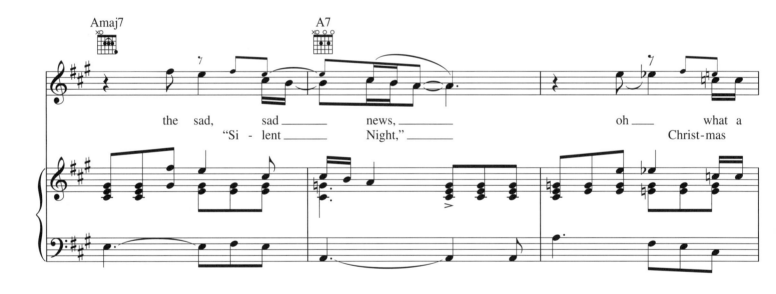

SWINGIN' THEM JINGLE BELLS

Music and Lyric by
JOHN HANCOCK

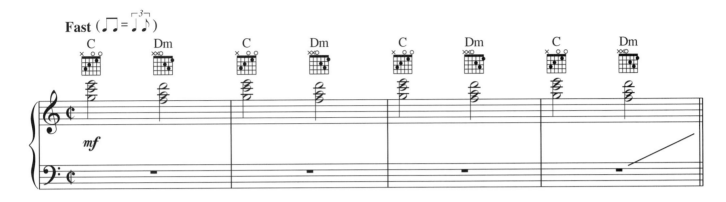

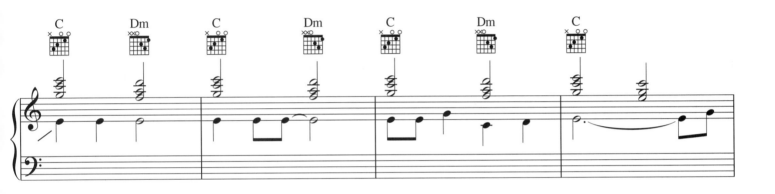

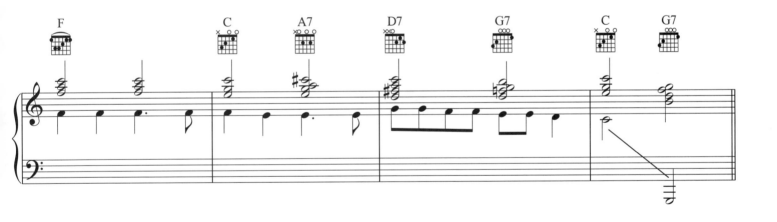

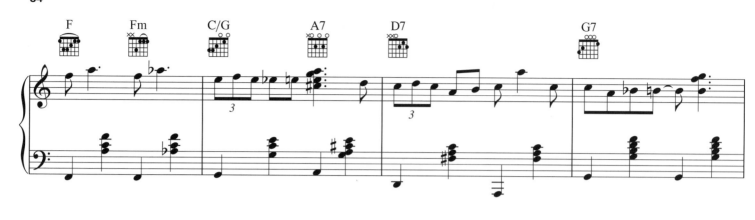

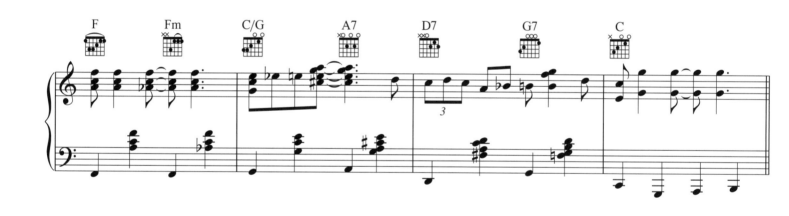

Jin - gle bells, jin - gle bells, jin - gle all the way.

SANTA BABY

By JOAN JAVITS,
PHIL SPRINGER and TONY SPRINGER

Moderately slow

Freely

Mis- ter "Claus," I feel as though I know ya, _____ so
you won't mind if I should get fa- mil- ya, will ya?

Moderately, with a relaxed beat

San- ta Ba- by, just slip a sa- ble un- der the tree ____
San- ta Ba- by, one lit- tle thing I real- ly do need;

SOULFUL CHRISTMAS

Words and Music by HANK BALLARD,
JAMES BROWN and ALFRED ELLIS

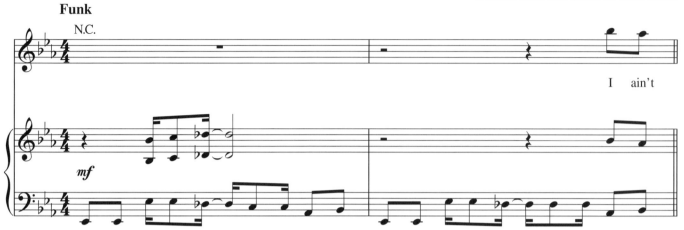

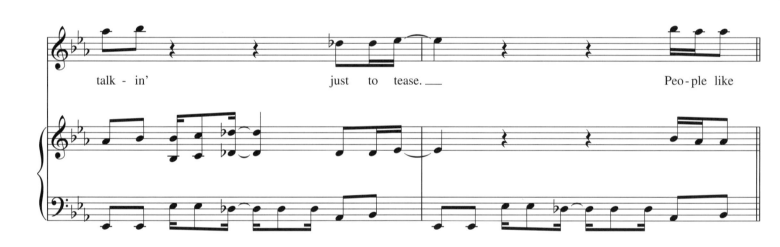

else _____
read - y

I can't stand my - self.
to bring the new year in.

Mer - ry Christ -

1 E9

Spoken improv: I got a mas.

2 E9

and a hap - py new

Eb7

year.

Repeat and Fade

T'WAS LOVE

Words and Music by
JANEY CLEWER

Turn down the

lights,   let the can-dle's light ___ in-spire ___
love   like a shin-ing star ___ to guide ___ me.

* Recorded a half step lower.

THIS CHRISTMAS

Words and Music by DONNY HATHAWAY
and NADINE McKINNOR

(1.,4.) Hang all the mis - tle - toe._ I'm gon - na get to know you bet - ter _____
(2.) Pres - ents and cards are here._ My world is filled with cheer and you, _____
(3.) *Piano solo ad lib.*

'ZAT YOU, SANTA CLAUS?

Words and Music by
JACK FOX

Is that you, __ San - ta Claus? __

Please, please, I prayed on my knees,

say that's you, __ San - ta Claus. _____

That's him alright.

Christmas Collections

from Hal Leonard
All books arranged for piano, voice & guitar.

All-Time Christmas Favorites – Second Edition
This second edition features an all-star lineup of 32 Christmas classics, including: Blue Christmas • The Chipmunk Song • The Christmas Song • Frosty the Snow Man • Here Comes Santa Claus • I Saw Mommy Kissing Santa Claus • Jingle-Bell Rock • Let It Snow! Let It Snow! Let It Snow! • Merry Christmas, Darling • Nuttin' for Christmas • Rockin' Around the Christmas Tree • Rudolph the Red-Nosed Reindeer • Santa, Bring My Baby Back (To Me) • There Is No Christmas like a Home Christmas • and more.
00359051...$12.95

The Best Christmas Songs Ever – 4th Edition
69 all-time favorites are included in the 4th edition of this collection of Christmas tunes. Includes: Auld Lang Syne • Coventry Carol • Frosty the Snow Man • Happy Holiday • It Came Upon the Midnight Clear • O Holy Night • Rudolph the Red-Nosed Reindeer • Silver Bells • What Child Is This? • and many more.
00359130...$19.95

The Big Book of Christmas Songs
An outstanding collection of over 120 all-time Christmas favorites and hard-to-find classics. Features: Angels We Have Heard on High • As Each Happy Christmas • Auld Lang Syne • The Boar's Head Carol • Christ Was Born on Christmas Day • Bring a Torch Jeannette, Isabella • Carol of the Bells • Coventry Carol • Deck the Halls • The First Noel • The Friendly Beasts • God Rest Ye Merry Gentlemen • I Heard the Bells on Christmas Day • It Came Upon a Midnight Clear • Jesu, Joy of Man's Desiring • Joy to the World • Masters in This Hall • O Holy Night • The Story of the Shepherd • 'Twas the Night Before Christmas • What Child Is This? • and many more. Includes guitar chord frames.
00311520...$19.95

Christmas Songs – Budget Books
Save some money this Christmas with this fabulous budget-priced collection of 100 holiday favorites: All I Want for Christmas Is You • Christmas Time Is Here • Feliz Navidad • Grandma Got Run Over by a Reindeer • Happy Holiday • I'll Be Home for Christmas • Jesus Born on This Day • Last Christmas • Merry Christmas, Baby • O Holy Night • Please Come Home for Christmas • Rockin' Around the Christmas Tree • Some Children See Him • We Need a Little Christmas • What Child Is This? • and more.
00310887...$12.95

The Definitive Christmas Collection – 3rd Edition
Revised with even more Christmas classics, this must-have 3rd edition contains 127 top songs, such as: Blue Christmas • Christmas Time Is Here • Do You Hear What I Hear • The First Noel • A Holly Jolly Christmas • Jingle-Bell Rock • Little Saint Nick • Merry Christmas, Darling • O Holy Night • Rudolph, the Red-Nosed Reindeer • Silver and Gold • We Need a Little Christmas • You're All I Want for Christmas • and more!
00311602...$24.95

Essential Songs – Christmas
Over 100 essential holiday favorites: Blue Christmas • The Christmas Song • Deck the Hall • Frosty the Snow Man • A Holly Jolly Christmas • I'll Be Home for Christmas • Joy to the World • Let It Snow! Let It Snow! Let It Snow! • My Favorite Things • Rudolph the Red-Nosed Reindeer • Silver Bells • and more!
00311241...$24.95

Happy Holidays
50 favorite songs of the holiday season, including: Baby, It's Cold Outside • The Christmas Shoes • Emmanuel • The First Chanukah Night • The Gift • Happy Holiday • I Yust Go Nuts at Christmas • The Most Wonderful Time of the Year • Silver Bells • Who Would Imagine a King • Wonderful Christmastime • and more.
00310909...$17.95

Tim Burton's The Nightmare Before Christmas
This book features 11 songs from Tim Burton's creepy animated classic, with music and lyrics by Danny Elfman. Songs include: Jack's Lament • Jack's Obsession • Kidnap the Sandy Claws • Making Christmas • Oogie Boogie's Song • Poor Jack • Sally's Song • This Is Halloween • Town Meeting Song • What's This? • Finale/Reprise.
00312488...$12.95

Ultimate Christmas – 3rd Edition
100 seasonal favorites: Auld Lang Syne • Bring a Torch, Jeannette, Isabella • Carol of the Bells • The Chipmunk Song • Christmas Time Is Here • The First Noel • Frosty the Snow Man • Gesù Bambino • Happy Holiday • Happy Xmas (War Is Over) • Hymne • Jesu, Joy of Man's Desiring • Jingle-Bell Rock • March of the Toys • My Favorite Things • The Night Before Christmas Song • Pretty Paper • Silver and Gold • Silver Bells • Suzy Snowflake • What Child Is This • The Wonderful World of Christmas • and more.
00361399 ....$19.95

FOR MORE INFORMATION, SEE YOUR LOCAL MUSIC DEALER, OR WRITE TO:

HAL•LEONARD® CORPORATION
7777 W. BLUEMOUND RD. P.O. BOX 13819 MILWAUKEE, WI 53213

Complete contents listings available online at www.halleonard.com

PRICES, CONTENTS, AND AVAILABILITY SUBJECT TO CHANGE WITHOUT NOTICE.

0808